This book is dedicated to

YOU and the magic pictures

within your imagination.

Illustrated by

| ME |
| At school |

What did you do in school today?

Nothing!

Nothing!

NOTHING YOU SAY!

Did you sit on yourself and stare at your chair? Did nothing

exciting happen there?

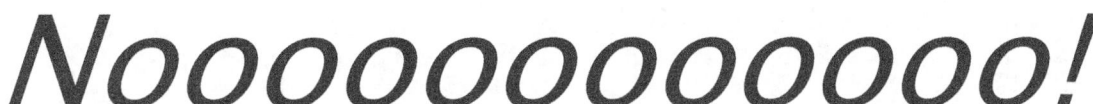

Nooooooooooooo!

Did a volcano blast up the teacher's desk?

Did the school bus driver pick up a bear?

Did a tiger jump from a lunchbox today

and eat a sixth grader there?

Did the custodian fly 'round the school

on a spoon...

or a 'hippo' get stuck in the girl's bathroom?

My, my, what a dull, dull day, to simply stare at yourself all day!

Did aliens attack the playground fair...

or a doo-doo bird pull the principal's hair?

Did lions jump o'er a python rope?

Did a dragon fall off the roof's steep slope?

Did you see any sharks eating cotton-candy

or monsters hanging from trees?

Were rabbits dodging colored eggs?

Now, that would surely please.

And what did you have for lunch, my child–

scrambled goose livers for a snack...

or monkey brains in chocolate sauce...

or fried fire crackers with Monterey Jack?

Did you munch on geckos with musubi?

How dull a day like that must be!

Did the substitute teacher have purple hair, or teach in some long underwear?

Was the school bus really a rocket ship, a technological blip, blip, blip...

That carried you off to another space

where weird things happened all over the place?

I'm sorry you had such a dull, dull day,

with nothing to see or do.

Who knows, but tomorrow will bring

a scene

that's not so dull for you.

Now, what would it be you'd like to see?

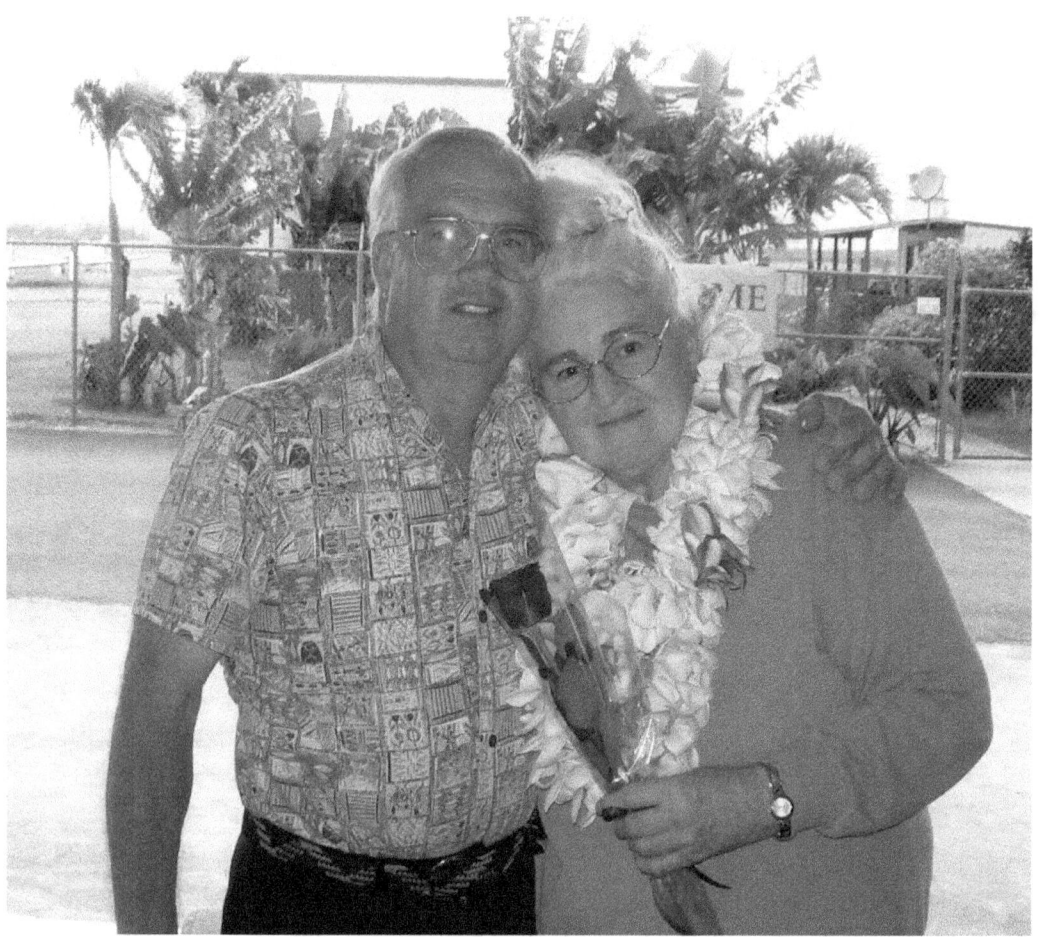

Susan Gerard–Schelinski lives with her husband, Jim, in Hawaii. Susan taught in Bellingham, Washington; Schoffield Barracks, Hawaii; Darrington, Washington; Lakewood, Washington; Kualapu'u, Hawaii; and Maunaloa, Hawaii.

This book was inspired by her grandson, who when asked, "What did you do in school today?", like many children encountered in years of teaching, always replied, "Nothing!" It was created for the hosts of creative children inhabiting classroom "boxes" and dulled by endless testing. May they ever know that great treasures lie within them as they think outside the box and delve into the depths of their imagination. To all you gifted children…happy illustrating!